Destiny in My Hands
PRIMROSE DZENGA

salmonpoetry

Published in 2010 by
Salmon Poetry
Cliffs of Moher, County Clare, Ireland
Website: www.salmonpoetry.com
Email: info@salmonpoetry.com

Copyright © Primrose Dzenga 2011

ISBN 978-1-907056-55-0

All rights reserved. No part of this publication may be reproduced or transmitted in any form or by any means, electronic or mechanical, including photography, recording, or any information storage or retrieval system, without permission in writing from the publisher. The book is sold subject to the condition that it shall not, by way of trade or otherwise, be lent, resold or otherwise circulated without the publisher's prior consent in any form of binding or cover other than that in which it is published and without a similar condition, including this condition, being imposed on the subsequent purchaser.

Cover artwork: **NYAKAMHIZA** by Gutsa
Cover design & typesetting: *Siobhán Hutson*
Printed by imprint*digital*.net

For my nieces Chiedza and Nyaradzo,
Who taught me how to love unconditionally,
giving me glimpses into motherhood,

To my mum, thank you, for always being there, you are a rock

Acknowledgements

Acknowledgements are due to the following publications, in which some of these poems first appeared:

"The Unsung Heroine" was published on the US Embassy website in March 2007. It has also been published in part by Zimbabwe Women Writers June 2009 in the book, *The Unsung Heroine*.

"If he made love" has been published in *The New Voices* magazine, November 2007. It has also appeared on Memory Chirere's Blog in December 2009 (www.kwachirereblogspot.com).

Contents

1. Haunting Destiny

Broken sentences	11
Whisper	13
Hush	15
Illusions	17
Midnight	19
Up down	20

2. Destiny Surreal

If he made love	25
Last Dance	27
Butterflies	28
If you were all I had	30
Love	31
Lustre in my petals	32
Personal demons	34
Twilight and dawn	35
Chinanazi	37
Colour my world	39

3. In My Hands, Destiny

Destiny in My Hands	43
The Unsung Heroine – Auxillia Chimusoro	44
Beauty in Vengeance	47
Caged	49
Chocolate queen	51
Dancing feet	52
Darkness within	53
If AIDS had a face	55
Lingerie	57
Prey	58

Deep in my sleep	60
Rain	62
The bashed queen and flowers	64
The damage we do our own	66
The weeping machete	68
These cuts	69
Wind, thunder and lighting	71

1.
Haunting Destiny

Broken sentences

Broken sentences, broken feelings, and half broken hearts
Strokes like the clock on the river of tumbling emotion
Repressed, oppressed in cascades under the skin

The itch at his finger tips
As he slides to caress that he wishes and despises to consume
Is he afraid?

Of demons lurking under his soul, under his feet
Beneath her skin
And veiled long lashes

Breathless emotions tumble
Mingled with drink, they are more intoxicating
The smell of her skin

He has to go, leave her, and leave them all behind
Running, sprinting in his mind, he must go
She is here, he has been running
Why does she follow?

She never moved
Sitting still, his blows to the heart in her eyes twinkle
Like a sorrowful widow
Pride holds her tears back

She smiles, he can't see
He has to run, from her, to her, all of them
Are they parting? Are they merging?

He sits in a bar corner
Butterflies in short pants wiggle and wink
So subtly serene it almost never was
A hassle free, no strings attached interlude, their wares on offer

How did she get into his beer?
Her veiled long lashes
Looking back from the glass thru swirls of beer
Her moans once again
Wrapped around him like a shawl

Walking out, walking away he knows
She will always be there
Right under his skin, so long as his owns heart beats

Whisper

As I rock, now in your arms and in my heart
Cry me a river, and drown me an ocean
For my heart is sunk and lost
It's drowned to depths unknown and told

I look into your eyes, I drown a million times
I watch you smile and die a million deaths
For I know now as I wallow
That this heart is dead to the world but you alone

Whisper your magic, your secret
That stole my heart like a thief at night
Made me dead to any other's touch
Untouchable, a statue a monument
Beautiful and unreachable

Now that my heart breaks, I'm bound and gagged
For sorrow and dejection
Others I have known and left
They have come and gone
With my blessings and blown kisses
A tear or two for company and farewell

Whisper my love, whisper, I need to know
So free and homeward bound I can set and glide
Free my heart and soul the core of me
I am bound and stuck by your magic

Let the magic words flow from your honeyed lips
Strong and beautiful, carved from stone
Your rib is strained and breaking
Set it free, by a few magic words
Only you can utter and set it loose

Like Noah's dove it will fly back
With an olive in its beak a smile of love and life
A promise for you and mankind
I love you today, tomorrow and forever
On you my heart, its roots and dregs I have poured
Whisper now, let me know and set me free

Hush

Hush my love
The sky in my stars
Don't let your heart groan so
Each time you moan
A gash stabs and tears through mine

My heart touches yours
Each moan, each cry and yearn
A sharp dagger, rending my heart

The comfort in knowing you know
Tenderness in your yearning and search
Such bitter sweet pain
A rosebud yet unblown
Now the bee can't suck

The sweet dew, like nectar
Like the lost bee I hover around thee
For the sweet nectar call from within

Were I free I wouldn't leave
Were I bound and gagged
Such gratitude would I render
For the promise, bittersweet
My yet unblown rose bud

Sleep now my love
Pray to fate
Woe lady destiny
Entreat her, for your sake and my own

Each step your feet
Each sob and weep our hearts
Each tear our souls
To one another cleave
Stronger, firmer than before

Open your heart to my own
As your cries lap my own
These enchantments from my heart
Lull you to slumber
My baby, my love
The first child to my heart
That will bless my soul with more

In a dream I see your smile
In your smile tears I discern
The look a royal falcon
Gracious yet so lonely
Your cup in overflow yet so empty
For what, you and I know

Hush now my heart
Let's solace in sleep, find
For in dreams we are one

Hush now dream weaver
Your yearning shatters my core
Your soul courts mine each night
Your spirit woes mine each hour
Don't cry so my heart

Sleep, peace and harmony
Eludes you and me
Hush now my soul

Listen to the music
Our heart beats
Like two larks in a groove
Hush now my love
Sleep and we will dream
Of parakeets gay and loud
Of our love merry and strong.

Illusions

I woke to a dawn misty and cloudy
Overcast hazy and shady
Wadding through the marches
Muddy traps of death
Gleaming, glittering and alluring

The wraiths and illusions
The loneliest place is a crowd I know
One full of beasts, wolves and tigers
Hungry, crouched, ready to pounce

Vampires, to suck my blood
All fair and pretty, sweet, sweet vampires
What to do, where to go, in a shoal of piranhas?
What I wouldn't give for a pod
One with a lonesome dolphin

Where have the angels gone?
The pure women of old
Who saw the man before the money?
That put and found the magic in love?
Oh where are the true maidens of old

That loved for love's sake
And saw the beauty, in a man's eyes
The depth and need of a mans heart
The gentle, firm maidens of old

All that's left now are illusions
Who do not kiss they bite
Who won't stroke they hit
That won't caress but scratch
That won't knead but pinch

Ah the firm maidens of old
Who bubbled like a Brooke?
And preened like pigeons
How I pray for one gentle maiden of old....

Midnight

I think of you at midnight
I dream of you awake at dawn
Conversations in a mystic tongue
Lie pearly jewels between you and me

What went wrong? What came between us?
I lie awake at night and caress the covers
I hear your raspy voice sleepy and potent
Chuckling cooing softly in my ear

You are my dream, do you know
My heart can't break; I know

My sixth sense coos and woes
The return of the king
Gentle spiritual lion king

But so much strength still
Like a woman I have felt
In touch with my land my destiny
Ah midnight passed an hour ago

Your raspy voice in my ear I miss
And your chuckles sleepy and warm
Your dreams and ideas into me poured

That's not all you will pour you know
Your essence and your soul as well
Your love for my love is yours and real

In yours I will rest, for a night, an eternity

I sleep and reach out for the dawn
And the potent yarn full of lure
Weaving itself around my heart
Stitching itself into my soul

Up down

Up down goes the see saw
Twirling, whirling, round and round
Through, forest, desert, rivers, fogs
Wondering, looking, searching
In moulds folded a ton

In mists, mystified by self
Shadows overshadowed in pain
Like the call of the wild
To the lonesome wolf
Up down still goes the see saw

In un-ending turn and churn
Of the wheel of lady fortune told
Round and unwound
In tales of fortune centuries old
And secrets timeless as sin
Up down still goes the see saw

Wishes dead and buried
On the eve of hope yet to be born
On the flimsy sleeve of a dare
A dare half heated and sickly
Thou hope will be born yet
Up down goes madam see saw

On fear, paranoia and unfounded
In memories of childhood anchored
In fears and trauma incomprehensible
To none save one who bore the brunt
Of trials devastating and crashing
Crippling the mind molding the body

Up down still goes the lady see saw
Of blood lost and innocence sapped
Trials of a world gone by and alive
It lives on in the bearer
A tale, a legend a myth
Very much alive and devouring

Thus the story sang and told
In word and verse
By the scribe, the jay
Singing for the voiceless
Seeing for the blind
Writhing the world in color
Like ivy and lilies in bloom
The dove that coos serene and tender

The eagle flapping and gliding high
The brave waterfall plunging
Plunging down, down and down some more
Down the cliff and jagged gorge
Up and down goes little madam see saw.

2.
Destiny Surreal

If he made love

(inspired by Trio ivoire-4 may HIFA 2007)

If he made love,
With such joy and abandon
Tenderness and care

If he caressed
Velvety feverish caresses
Like he did the cords,
Sweet cords of his piano

And revered, with lavished concern
Like he did, the wide amble bosom
Of his lady marimba churning
She, creaking and groaning
To the fevered touch and pitch
Of a practiced master in love

My soul was a virgin
Till the echoes of his drums
The wailing and moaning of his piano
The sheer joy and celebration
Of his marimba in love.

Awoke my spirit to canal desires
Unquenchable lust and need
For more of this music
This melody and joy
Making love to my soul

Peeling away the blinds and mists
Of naivety, being green
My soul was sated, sated to voluptuousness
But now….? I'm sated no more
Im addicted to the quick

For the hunger now gnaws
Craving, the wails, the echoes and ululations of joy
In their chosen trio on a journey
Have left a hunger I could never quench

The melodies wafting thru me
Taking me, my spirit on a journey
Pitting me with the moon
For a dance under the African sky

If he made love
Like he massaged the piano
And smiled into the marimba
And tickled his drums to fits

There would be no more need for love
All would be sated like I was
But I'm sated no more
So I beg you, play on.
With your three ladies of choice

You bring out the best in them
And springs of joy to the world
Initiating most, to a higher level
Of appreciating music and nature

If he made love
Like they did to the three
Conceiving such sweet melodies
I beg you gentlemen, please
Make some more, do make some more.

Last Dance

let me kiss your nose
for i know its the last time
let me hold you to my heart,
for it aches and pains
maybe this once the void you can fill

let me smell your hair
its musky and sweet
i see tears in your heart
for your eyes are hidden
i hear the wails in your chest ,
for they are in mine too

i wish to touch your skin,
but i can touch your soul
i wish to kiss your lips
but i kiss your heart
for there is always a place for you and me
where no one else can see,
where you and i can go

i wish for a waltz and a hug
the ballroom's too big and too noisy
the dance floor too busy,
no space for you and me

i cant whisper into your ear,
i can sing to your heart
for your heart and mine knows ,
that this is true
and we will call it our last dance ?
for i love you so much it hurts.......

Butterflies

Frozen, out of reach, intangible
Love is like ice in a glass
So pale, hard, cold and small

Around it we float
In swirls, whorls and circles
Like butterflies by a flower in glass

Enslaved, chained by nostalgia
Of what the heart knows
The body will never reach
What telepath and empathy revels in

Like butterflies we float
Bumping into our own reflections
Mirrored in time by glass
The glass housing she
The mystique of all time,
Love

Like fervent butterflies we hover
With hope and determination
Stirred by the heart, who won't die?

Who demands life by the blood?
Of love in the glass
A frozen cube without thaw
Who will thaw and mock it
At every touch of the lips

Once again you can't feed
Loves mocks you,
Like a maiden in bloom
Thus around her we hover,
For eternity, like butterflies by the glass

The glass that bears she
The flower of our hearts
Elusive, eternal, surreal,
Love

If you were all I had

If you were all I had
In these sun kissed arms
And weather beaten brow

Like a lone star,
Capped in haunting twinkle
At midnight through the clouds

A lone pebble by the beach in sparkle
Through the sand like a diamond
Lonesome and whole

Would I pass you by, would I hold you?
Would I, stumble through
My nightmare perfumed dreams?

To hunger caressed thoughts
And sun kissed, fanned yearning?
And yearning withered desires
Of love hugged dreams

Would I undress to reach?
And bare all?
Cobwebs,
Cloistering my heart and thoughts?

Haunting in dreams, in loss
Creeping shadows holding me back by shards
Splintering in pieces, like glass this veil
My womanhood and thoughts

If you were all I had
Like a lily, I would smile still,
Reach and enfold your blooms
In this my secret, most primal warmth

Love

Have I head love?
Whispering in my ear? Smelt love?
Breathed love in sweet torrents like perfume?
Does it have a scent?
Have I dreamt love?

Ominous like the moon
Gleaming, glinting like stars
Have I ever felt the moon?
Gently brush against my soul?

Have I ever cuddled in embrace stars?
Have I felt love then?
Touched love?
Embraced and enfold it?

In my arms like a baby
In my dreams, like a sorcerer?
And draw its gentle smell like a cloud?
Or is it imagination?
Veering and wafting in clouds…

Lustre in my petals

This shield of lustre in my petals
The smoke screen and mirage
Like a fog, mystical mist
To all secrets of my soul

So fragile and petite
Like a tingling Chinese vase
Don't crush me with your big hands
And Squeeze my petals to waste

And lay waste all the sap
That renders them velvety perfumed
Tainting your hands with stains
Stains of a too fragile soul
The life blood of the wild rose

Don't crush me with your big feet
As I sway and swoon by the wayside
Just a wild flower in bloom
Meant to perfume the wilderness
And render it sweet in its savagery

Like a little rabbit in the thicket
Wild yet scared
Like the scattering petals
Of golden flowers of the wild

Whose softness reflects?
Velvety softness reveals
The soul hidden behind the big face
The big hands and feet
The gigantic frame and carriage
All souls and hearts are gentle in side

Hidden, covered in wilderness of nurture
Like the swooning little lady
Wild golden flower, by the wayside.
Don't crush my little petals in your wake
I only wish to perfume,
That which the lord made gentle to preserve

Personal demons

Days, weeks, months and years go bye
Dreaming of another life, gone yonder
To a place of no salvage, no return

Like a torn cloth I watch agape
Holding the exorcism torch high above
Is it over or in my head?

Was my heart involved or was i dreaming
Or is it still? I wonder a while,
Behind these cliffs of silence I sit

And wait for the fogs to clear
So I can tell the sun and moon apart
Exorcising personal demons!!!!!

Twilight and dawn

Each twilight and dawn
Day mocks nightfall
Victory at hand
Abundant spoils of war

Plundering, ransacking and seizing
With joy, glazes and glare
He won't traverse my territory ever
Hence exile me to oblivion
Shrouded, adorned in darkness

Like a maze puzzled in churn
Of the wheels of time in turn
History reborn, the old hag story
Over and over again told

Nightfall on the horizon knocks
And I wait for tomorrow, sunrise
To mock and puzzle
By the twilight at dawn

With night darkness in retreat
When you glare at noon
The fort to reclaim
And scorch all in wrath
In wide tides like the sea

Weeding out the root and anchor
Of night and darkness's descent
The final lock and key
To the mortal enemy's fortress

The puzzle and mazes of time
The labyrinth of creation
The unknown, invisible clock above
The hand of wind and rain

Always watching and knowing
Like a cheater waylaying prey
The mazes and puzzles of time
Tomorrow will turn again
With twilight and dawn

Chinanazi

(Wild Pineapple)

Oh my wild pine apple?
Double edged
Like a spear without a handle
Waves in the wind, my owl's feather

You wring my heart
You tickle my lungs
You have given me stitches in my thoughts,
My mouth is now dry, dry like a desert palate

My mind in swirls and twirls
Like a sparrow hawk in the sky
My heart is scotched and withered
A dead bream the pool surface

My wild pine apple? With shimery shiny thorns?
The dove and thorns of my heart
In your shade lamely I sit
With my heart in my mouth
Like a lost toad by the riverside
Im in overfill I can't sit still
Like a poisoned fish by the bank

Oh my…How do I hold you now?
Oh thorny, Peerless, faultless darling
My falcon feather,
Jealously guarded by a mamba?

You have plucked my heart
You have tortured and tormented me sweet apple
And drowned my soul to depths unknown and told
Where the rabbit went so the dog followed
And none came back…

You have sifted my marrow and broken all my bones
How do I scratch this itch? The itch in my heart?
Plastered on your smooth shiny skin?
Velvety, black and smooth like African wild berries?

Pine apple of my sore eye
Whose teeth are white and gleam like stars?
Whose eyes blur my mind's eye?
You have done me in, tormented me sweet apple
You have roasted me inside out like corn
And ground me in a mortar into a fluffy ball
Now I wallow in ashes and mud like a mule

There is no more day no more night
Happiness and sorrow are now pot and pitcher
I can't watch the sunset no more
Im just sitting here by the shade
The shade of thorns
Thorns of my heart, you wild pine apple.

Translated from the original shona poem "Chinanazi" by Primrose C Dzenga

Colour my world

Mauve, golden, violet and primrose
The rainbow and sunshine
Misty fine showers off the cove
The cove, the core of my heart

You colour my world
All the rainbow colours
With reds so impassioned and flushed
Creams and whites pure and true
Blues soft and tender
Tender like your heart and bosom

In purples regal and stately
With rich red of orchids
That whisper of love and passion
That intoxicates the eye, soul and heart

When you colour my world
Nothing else compares
No one else in your stead would stand
Nor anything would I hold dearer
Not even my life's worth
For what would my life be?
Without light, colors, and passion?

You seat and weave at night
Spells to take my breath away
Dream weaver, my love
Enchant me, ensnare me some more

If this be hell and purgatory,
Heaven shall I never wish to behold
Like the sunset you glow
With the sunrise you blink and glitter

Jasmine never smelt sweeter
Than you my love at dawn
Roses never looked lovelier
Than you my love at night
Carnations never looked elegant
By you my love at noon

Lilies never looked prettier, lovelier
Than you my love in the rain
Nor hyacinth more resilient
Than you my love in woes

Now that you colour my world
Don't fade with the sunset
Dream weaver, my love
Don't you wax and wane
Like stars at night
Don't glitter in puddles
Like a diamond in the rough

Should you fade and go my love,
You fade with my heart and soul,
With you I will be lost and gone
Colour my world some more
For a day, a year, a decade`
all eternity will come and pass
I will swim and wallow in you, my world

3.
In My Hands, Destiny

Destiny in My Hands

Do you mock me, fair one?
Do you insult me whirlwind of worlds unknown?
Or do you try and tempt me?
Now in my hand you repose
Temperate lady destiny?

Destiny in my hands
Fair as a shell conch
In my hand, my heart my being
So fine, too thin to tread,
The line I can feel and not see
Yet too wide to leap,

Hence destiny must I embrace
A chaste peck on the cheek
Formal, stone cold, dead
Dare I enfold and entangle
In my arms, my life, my emotions?
My heart, my dreams and fantasy,

The Unsung Heroine – Auxillia Chimusoro

What legacy surpasses life?
What more would one ask a parent?
Let alone a stranger, a sister
Opening her own wounds

Bleeding for you and me
Bleeding for her very torturers?
Bleeding, for many generations to come?
Telling the world
A community, whose bosom is bare,
Like the barren womb of a mare
Of pity, of understanding, of acceptance?

That she bears, the apparition, that feasts,
On you and me?
On our blood rich and sweet
On our lives young and promising
On our youth succulent and tender
On our old gracious and wise
On our continent age old and rich

AIDS bled her a little, for a pillar she was
But what little or more it left
Of her courageous blood
We, with out tongues, and empty   hearts bled
With taunts, teases, hisses, and slander
Of the woman, the one woman
Who came out of the gale like a pillar?
Who stood to weather your storm and mine

So your apparition could be treated like any other
So you children can stand up and say
Im positive and live positively
I have AIDS but I'm alive!!!!

Who stood up and said enough!
To dying quietly like a lamp
Who unselfishly sacrificed her peace?
Her privacy and her life, a few more days at least
For though she fought
Every jab, of stigma and hate
A second away took
From that life, the strong fighting woman

Nehanda was a heroine,
We sing and praise her
Why not Auxillia, Our unsung heroine?
Africa is at war, Zimbabwe more so

Not a war with guns
But at war with disease
And she was a general
Tireless, fearless,
Resourceful, graceful and strong
A tigeress, a true daughter of Africa

A true mother, sister, fighter and friend
A shameful waste and pity
If we sleep and forget
That today I got ARVS
Yesterday I got support
A shoulder to cry on
A forum to air my views,
Pains and tribulations

Snore and forget
Before the rainbow came a storm
The storm rages on but the sun shone
With hope and strength,
Formidable and undaunted
As none other than she
The true unsung heroine
Of modern day Zimbabwe

A light, a torch, a luminary
Out of Africa, for Africa
For I say Africa is at war
War with disease and famine
And its time we all sing
Our unsung heroes and heroines

Like she
A true daughter and fighter
Against AIDS, against ignorance
Against stigma, and
Against death by good measure
May her soul rest in peace!!!!

A tribute to Zimbabwe's most formidable daughter against AIDS/HIV and stigmatization

Beauty in Vengeance

Have you ever beheld?
A flower in second bloom
Prime and mature
With velour and aroma
Spicy, sweet and wild

The shy buds now wither
Dry petals kiss its feet
All dried and withered
Of last season's sun

Now watch beauty in vengeance
The vengeance of second bloom
The avengers of beauty and bloom
Strengthened by beauty and pain

The buds so strong and bold
No longer shy and sweet
But alluring and delicate
Like the jelly fish sting
So harmless yet so dangerous

The allure of a desert sunrise
The sun will bloom and you wither too
As the beauty grows and avenges
The chills and stars of the night gone by

Yet you wither and adore the sun still
As your lips crack and you ask for more
Provocatively you lick the lips
And the sun kisses you more
As its true beauty reposes
On you and all around

The sand bakes and kisses you too
Like the mighty flower
Mighty flower in second bloom
Behold the bees in dance and song
As they sing for the second bloom

And sap its nectar contend
Satisfying, heavy and sweet
On this flower they shall dance
And kiss the buds in bloom

Caged

I look out the window, I feel caged
Ensnared, imprisoned like a bird
In walls so thick so dark yet transparent

From my perch I can hear, I can see
The coo of the night dove
Alone by my window sill

The echoes of his lonely cry
Shattering, tearing away my soul
My heart, my fear
With hunger, incessant want and need

For freedom, for peace, mediocrity
Then I see, I realize, I wake up
This cage, this prison, these walls

Paper thin walls binding my hands, my growth, my life,
Paper thin walls blinding my vision
Paper thin walls in fear encased

Paper thin walls strong as steel
Transparent walls, chiding, teasing with
With what's denied me

Like a caged bird I flutter and flounder
Crying for freedom, for peace just fresh air
Crying, weeping just to be

Like a horn bill I'm tired, I'm done
Flowing with this wind, tossing, twisting me
Blowing me everywhere taking me nowhere

I must break free

I must fly out, tear this cage to shreds
And so should you, every one
Destroy these paper thin walls

Running away with my, life, my dreams
And yours
From my perch, I see, I realize
A generation, a host of prisoners

Like me, caged in comfort zones
Staying in one hell lest the next one is hell too
Can't we laugh? Can't we cry? Can't we smile?
Cant we walk, talk, love and laugh in peace?
Can't we break these walls?

And live just one day?
Free of fear, free, just free and head someplace
Hell or heaven does it matter?
Hell is, I feel caged.
In this paper thin cage.

Chocolate queen

The chocolate queen ice quoted
Melting inside frozen all round
A molten Madonna ready to explode
But all still thought
Behold the ice queen

Is that sweet?

Dancing feet

Gyrating in rhythmic course
Wild blood coursing through these veins
Beating the earth like drums in tune

Acoustic tunes of a world gone by
Of ancient graves and secrets untold
Of old women pregnant

With rhythm, graceful dignity
Bearing secrets, of forests, woods and caves
Of riches guarded by patterns traced in sand

Their dancing feet a key
In a maze, treasure hunts of self
Of a people of a time
Of a song

Dancing feet, quiet, serene in their allure
Flirting with chants, trances to a hidden past
Of wealth in caves, plains and pools

Of ivory, of gold of copper
Strewn on this path, dancing feet
To acquire beads for the curvaceous she

These feet, dancing feet, carry the key
To treasures, pleasures and surrender
To the motherland untold

Darkness within

If you only knew,
It's the darkness within
That consumes and destroys
And spreads like a cancer
From the core to the skin

Till your tongue
Your words, your being
Turn to poison that festers like a wound
In self destruction all lights to banish

Now the morning lark flies
To a place of dawns bright and mauve
With sunsets chiming
The clocks of time in grind
Others don't fight your war

Support and strength they render
The final step, and tread, in your breast lays anchored
Like a beacon in gloom shadowed
The light within
With ambers bright, gold and warm

All gone and lost now
Consumed, tainted
Poisoned, corrupted
Prostituted and enslaved

The stray path not quite lost
Another life, another destiny
In this tale of fates
Crossed, bestowed and lost

The secret passage to follow
In which lies the chords
To eternal felicity
Of souls intertwined

Now the jay can only sing
And light bloom like roses
The mourning widow of destiny

Off she flies...no more tears to weep
On a leaf to patch
And beckon to your heart

To see thru your soul
What the eyes slept on
The breast feels and knows

If AIDS had a face

If AIDS had a face, a life to live
What would it look like? Would it look like?
A journey? Long winding, sad or merry
Would it twist in swirls, turning back, forth and about?

Would it look like a lion roaring tearing the jungle to shreds?
Destroying and devouring all in its path?
a leopard, sneaky and slimy, sucking our life blood
The blood of generations, over centuries built?
A tiger uncompromising, aggressive treading us to dust

Or would it look like an alien
A monster tearing through this forest our lives?
Or that girl next door? The friend next to you?

The love of your life, your dreams come true and more?
The men next door, the mother next door
Their cousin next door
Perhaps, just a problem next door

Yet we perish each day, on all five faces of lady earth
Neither water, ice nor sun a barrier enough
In its silver jubilee of dominance and destruction
Of hunting and preying effectively
On our youth and life blood

I still wonder, If AIDS had a Face
What would it look like? Would it push love asunder?
When to crouches and sinks its tentacles,
Through your softest spot, your heart your love
To destroy, in havoc, in fear and undignified pain

Now I recall from a dream of one tear too many
From sorrows of one loss too many
If AIDS had a face it would look, like me, like my brother
My sister, my cousin, my whole family, like you and your family

Yes it would look like all of us
We are the face of AIDS, and its time we accept the challenge
Destroy it, so when we wake tomorrow
A free generation and the true face of survival and victory.
We present to mother earth and stars shining galore

Lingerie

Woven intertwined like yarn
Blushing rose, petals
Dew strewn at dawn

Never saw, the light of day
Glistening of the moon shy
Beauty of night, sparkling stars
Like faraway diamonds hung

Lingerie of the soul
From prying eyes, hidden
A bathing suit, to the painter's core

Would I let you see?
Holes, patches in my soul?
Peep-holes to my core
Vulnerable in its nakedness

The world will never glimpse
The best poetry there ever was
Save a pair of eyes
Taken glimpses into windows
Windows, of the soul.

Prey

Sleek car, pink and brown face, golden mane
Come to the dumping ground down town to hunt
For us the "menace" urchins of the street

Promises of a huge feed
Clean sheets and good money
It will buy food for a day
That's rich, I can't resist

If you starve sunset to sunrise
And hug sewer pipes each night
And face hostile looks everywhere you go.

Oh and a wash too
Before he bends me every which way
To partake of my small body all his joy and desire
Sadistic whip lashes
Grunting like a pig
Oblivious to my wails and moans
To this violation of body and soul

It's the thick black jungle
Bam! In the midst of this city
Of glitz glamour and shame
I must survive I'm a lion too

As he preys on me
Night after night
I will prey on them
Day after day

Grabbing chains, watches of gold
Do they ever wonder?
Where their gold goes?

Just to another shark
Another lion
Preying on my too fragile belly
And instinct for survival

Real lions are sleek
Im just a buck
To use as they will.

Deep in my sleep

Knocked on my door, deep in my sleep
Spangled mane and locks, the phantom destiny
Lions roar in splendor and pride

A glimpse into the future
The double bundle in store
Fate and destiny twists so
Crossed me oceans and took me back

To the land, fruits and restoration
Where providence lie engraved
So I stare, impatiently below
At the yet un-dried butterfly, wriggling out in folds
Sculptured and molded in the cocoon
Dare I alter fate, dare I alter destiny?

Like a wheel in churn and turn
On the eve of destiny ride
To see the prophecy fulfilled
Carried in dreams, buoyed in veins

Can I rub out what she carved?
To muddle and puddle
With vehicles, vessels, of fate
The lion will roar and strut awhile

The queen rules the pride
By the token she hunts and nurtures
On milk bourne of blood and death,
Warrior queen, whose arm nurtures and kills
Like the Nile in flood, killing and healing

The fertility goddess gleaming
Outdoes all harvests gone by
This double bundle, like two peas in a pod,
The harvest, the prophecy
Good and hard times to come
Just a prophecy fulfilled.

Rain

Hail storm, a child's experience

"Where are you mummy its raining snow white pebbles?" I hear huge deafening noises outside, and a smell like the river close by. Mummy has gone somewhere, I want to go out and pick the white little Blocks falling

Pitter patter with my little feet
Mummy must know what I'm about to do
I think it s not allowed
I have to pick some of those

I step out side and I'm bitten by little pebbles all over, I try to look up but they bit my eyes and I can't see. I call out to mum as I blindly feel for the door with my outstretched hands. Another clap of the deafening noise and I cover my ears. Mum can't hear me now, but I don't know that. Putting out my hands to feel the walls I stray further and further.

The pebbles wont stop hitting me maybe it's the boys next door. Last time they killed my cat with a catapult now they want to finish me. No matter how loud I scream, these drums from the, sky drown my voice. I can even hear some hosho Can't they see I'm being murdered? Yet they dance and play drums up there in the skies.

I stop moving I'm tired, I'm ready to die. I can't even close my mouth these pebbles hurt.

Plonk!!One falls into my mouth
Its cold and bitter sweet
I should open my mouth a little more

Plonk Plonk, Plonk
I got three this time
What if I put out my tongue too?

Plonk, ah that hit my lip
I start dancing and jumping out
My eyes shut against the pebbles
My mouths open to capture the little white pebbles

They taste like ice-cream
Ice-cream without sugar.
I stopped crying a long while ago, I don't even know when the pebbles stopped falling and my mum came out. I'm sore but happy. My eyes are blood shot and I'm being scolded. I will have to change and wash but listen to the frogs in my favorite pond. They must have been singing to my dancing all along.

The bashed queen and flowers

Black, bartered blue and purple eyes
Flowing tears, like wild brooks bubbling
With sorrow pain and abuse
From the other half of me, my spouse

Of misconstrued love, hatred, insecurities
A dozen roses for a dozen fists
A dozen, boots a dozen punches a dozen graves

Of women clutching love at the recesses of their soul
Misguided dignity and endurance
What dignity is there in shame?

In abuse and torture, unreasonable jealousy
"Dzokera kumurume mwanangu, ndozvinoita dzimba"
"Go back little one that's what marriage is like"
Chorusing my aunt, my grandmother, my mother

I wish to run, to scream and spit on this hell
To run away from his fists, stand up by walking away
I'm trapped, caged like a bird,
I see the rainbow, just outside, what good is it?
I'm drenched; I'm soaked to the soul, I'm frozen

Behind the door I seat, in dread of his
Drunken tread and sway
Clutching to the breast my little girl
Lest I'm bashed before she suckles for the night

On my face his fist tread, splitting my lips knocking my teeth
In frenzy my eye goes, so does my rib, and my arm
Like a broken bird, I crumble, crumble to an early grave

A heap of broken bones and blood
As I drift away in pain and sorrow
Of love abused, misused misconstrued and betrayed
To a grave dug long ago,
When I took the first punch and stayed

Leaving my seven children orphaned and homeless
The 16 v murdered him too
Two strangers, two graves, seven orphans
To you I cry from beyond my grave

Don't wait for death in abuse
Nor for love turned sour, violent and foul
Jealousy is not love, a fist does not pat
Nor does a boot caress……..

The damage we do our own

Moans and whimpers whispers of agony
Sighs, of death gruesome and inhuman
Ruthless butcher of men women and children

Waste of infants in cradles
Wretched out of their mother's arms
Torn from the mothers breast
A nipple torn and stuck
Between the cold toothless gums
Of the sweet innocent infant or is it still?
Lays beside the mother

Oh what mother dare you speak of now?
Only a headless heap of flesh
Rotting and wasting
Amidst a feast of maggots and flies
Amidst chaos and debris

Who is the enemy now
What war is this ?
Whose war ?why this mindless killing
Oh Africa behold and awake
We kill our own and skin them alive

Oh the dawn is bloody
For gallons have been spilt this night
By us skinning our own
With mindless brutality,
Of beasts of the wild
In heartless massacre and torture
Behold the women and children
The beauty and milk of our land

Lying in rot and waste
By our own hand and cold hearts
The boy crawls down the street
For his leg is now no more
Rummaging through debris
Searching for what once was
The precious family of mixed blood
That gave him the world

Oh a world that's gone mad, wild and buried
For the father mutilated the mother
Purifying blood, purging the land of vermin
In racial cleansing, amazing barbarity
Vermin! of the one that gave you love and care

The damage we do our own
Only we can say enough!!!!
Wake up this night and say no
Restore the dawn and a sunrise
And the coral black night diamond studded
No more killing no more war
Oh awake Africa and behold
The damage we do to our own!!!!

The weeping machete

I'm past sobbing I weep
Too much tears, too many victims
Too many lives lost,

I the machete weep
For the abuse and sin befalling me
Im tired cutting I have to slice

Blood of innocence, blood of villains
Their blood my tears
On my cold flat cheeks stick and cloat

Sometimes I pucker, the tears come still
I know not why they induce
These red tears now freely frolicking

On my flame kissed lips
And hammer teased cheeks
To take away the glint and life
The beauty I once possessed

I had shine I was sharp
Now I weep tears
Tears of blood
Blood of innocence

Like an old hag I weep
With bitterness, I'm helpless
Blood trickles down this blade

With the lost lives I weep
These blood tears taint and cleanse
The untold pain I behold

These cuts

These cuts across my back
tattoos, of those that bore me
The stamp of my people
The essence of Africa
Dancing across my back
In swirls, whorls and patterns

tattoos across my back
Lovingly etched, edged and designed,
In my flesh like clay
With the love and accuracy of a master
By the guardians of she
Wise old women of Africa

The guardians of the essence
The essence of the mahogany queen
Splaying across these two mountains
Designing the valley with ridge and contour
Polishing the curves on my back
Decorating to allure and preserve

Dainty little pieces of china
These cuts, dancing across my back
With essence and fever
More pitched and potent
To surpass the reed dance of old

These patterns and tattoos
That carry my name to the soil
And my womanhood above
To the ones who went before me

The stamp of the old mother
Whose offspring are dwindling fast?
Into ignorance and mayhem
Endangered and extinct

With these cuts, splayed across my back
Proud and tall I stand
A giraffe across the African plain
The striped zebra in cantor
To the river to smell the mud and essence

Of womanhood and all our mothers hold dear
Of pleasure and all our men hold sacred
Of fertility and the breast our children will suck
Of power we all carry in our waists
Of the matriarch revered in awe

Imbued in these cuts
Age old secrets buried in each one
Of these cuts, sacred little tattoos,
Dancing across my back

Wind, thunder and lighting

Life is wind, thunder and lighting
A flower, blowing, swaying in the storm
Hurled from one boulder to another

Passed from stream to stream
On wings of currents
Torrents, washing to the end

Endless pattering raindrops
Lighting and thunders
Perfumes of grooves, hurled and torn

Screams, screeches, of creatures trampled
Song, dance and twitters
Of the muddy frog next door

Storms and clouds wafting by
Peering sands, whirlwinds of time
Nomadic pendulum, these dunes
Like a song

No dancer, no music, just rhythm
Wind, rain and thunder
This, passage of time
Life, the wind.